BUILDING A HEALTHY RELATIONSHIP

Simple things to do in a relationship than love

MAXWELL COLLINS

Table of contents

CHAPTER SIX

INTRODUCTION

It is very easy to get caught up in strong feelings for others. After all, love is a powerful cocktail of emotions, and it may seem like that's what really matters...but there are some things that matter more in relationships than love. And it's important to keep these things in mind when moving forward as a couple. But that doesn't mean you can't be totally romantic at the same time. And nothing beats receiving flowers from your loving partner. These are great add-ons. Cute things you do for each other to show how passionate you are. But just like your giant heart-shaped eyes, they don't bring you together. When it comes to love and relationships, everything is much more complicated.

Trust, respect, good communication and much more must be done. Otherwise, it's not. It can become stale and even toxic over time. If you actively seek out these other elements, it will create a stronger foundation for the relationship to last.

CHAPTER ONE

Trust each other

No matter how much you love someone, if you can't trust them, it won't work. Trust is essential to a healthy relationship. As such, he is always one of the first things professionals look for when evaluating a couple's relationship. We're not just talking about cheating or infidelity, but trusting confidential information, trusting vulnerability, trusting them to get through tough times, etc. It's all about your partner having your back and you have his back. Without trust, you will lead a life of stress and hurt. Do you want to spend your days dealing with the nagging worries that come with a dubious or unavailable partner? Make faith your goal because it's not the way to live. If you can't achieve it right away, you can do it over time, perhaps with the help of a therapist. Consider ways to build trust.

Be respectful

Have you ever had or seen this conversation? "My partner is so stupid." "So why are you with them?" "Because I love her." This classic exchange shows how love can blind you to the reality of bad situations, including the fact that you're with someone who doesn't respect you. The thought of breaking up, and the thought of losing someone you love sounds absolutely miserable, it makes you want to look the other way. Please remember how respectful you are. Respect is about respecting each other's differences. "Couples don't have to share the same interests or passions, but they do need the ability to understand each other",

"You must be with your partner - no judgments, demands, or unattainable expectations."

Forgiveness

Forgiveness is a very important virtue and no one in this world is perfect. You may have a list of qualities you want in a partner but at the end of the day, it is human to make mistakes and Forgiveness is God. Once you've sincerely apologized, learn to forgive and move on. However, cheating on your partner is not allowed. But some unfortunate mistakes and subsequent apologies are conceivable.

Respond emotionally

A relationship is about love and happiness, but it's also about being emotionally available to your partner during difficult times. Listen when your partner wants to be heard about emotional issues. She is her insensitivity to her emotions and loss in her own world can entice her partner to fill it up in the third person. Listening to and acknowledging your partner's feelings makes you closer and stronger as a couple.

CHAPTER TWO

Be Kind

The small gestures of kindness you do to your partner may seem small, but they will be remembered forever. These small gestures can show your partner that you care about them and that you always support them. And rest assured that they will do their best to reciprocate those acts of kindness in their own way to make you feel special. This lays the foundation for a serious relationship.

Commitment to Success

Every relationship is a two-way street and for it to work it needs two people who are committed to each other. If you are invested in your relationship it will survive any hardships. Relationships have their challenges, and those who survive the ravages of time have a commitment as a key factor. It may shock many, but love is not the only wish for a happy and fulfilling relationship. It consists of many small but important components. Open communication, loyalty, kindness, compassion, trust, emotional vulnerability, and a willingness to forgive are some of the most important things to maintain in a relationship. The partner in you cares most about feeling secure, while others may rely heavily on respecting each other's boundaries.

Security and safety

Do you feel safe or secure in your relationship? If the

answer is no, it doesn't matter how much you love the person. Especially if you're in an emotionally abusive relationship. A toxic situation is a toxic situation, no matter how you try to frame it. But when you focus solely on love, it can be really hard to see. Of course, these types of relationships can be more sticky because one or more of your unique needs are met, you'll probably keep it. Love can satisfy many needs, such as the need for validation, support, and connection. When toxic situations arise, it's often best to look for safer ways. Love alone is not enough to fix an emotionally abusive partner, no matter how hard you try.

Work on your overall well-being as a couple

Everyone wants to be happy, and happiness is really important - it's not always happy. In fact, it's normal to be unhappy for a long time, especially if you're dealing with a crisis. But happy times should come first when you add up happy times and unhappy times. Even in the most loving and head-to-head relationships, this takes work. We need to keep learning from each other, including sharing our hopes, dreams, and fears. It is very important to understand what drives your partner into their life and how that changes over time. You can also give it a boost. Love is one thing, but when you really support each other, you really feel like you have a partner. And what could be better than that?

CHAPTER THREE

Genuinely liking each other

Staying in a relationship with someone you don't actually like just because you love them is more common than you might think. If you don't get it, think of a family member who is always criticizing you or who doesn't get along with you. You love them because they are family, but you don't really like being around them. The same thing happens with your partner. You may love them very much, but you hate spending time together, not making each other laugh, and not having anything in common. So if things get stale, be careful. You can't force yourself to like someone, but you have to build and maintain an ongoing sense of connection. It's about taking a genuine interest in who your partner is, who they want to be, and how they can find common interests and connections.

Maintain self esteem

You were you before we were and you need to remain you when you enter a relationship. No love is worth giving up on the essence of who you are. Losing yourself, forgetting your own interests, giving up on your goals is a problem. It's not necessarily a deal breaker, and it's not the relationship's (or your partner's) fault. But you should try to hold onto the basic truth about who you are. By working with your partner to make time for the things that are important to you, and encouraging your partner to do the same, you can reclaim yourself. Were you in the middle of writing a book? Have you trained for a half marathon? Encouraging each other to return to their hobbies and interests actually leads to a greater sense of love and a more meaningful relationship.

Keep your independence in a relationship

Similarly, in relationships, it is not only important to be free to do what you want, to be yourself, to go anywhere and have your own thoughts and feelings, it is essential. By losing for the sake of loving, you are actually doing her a disservice. You can (and should) involve your partner in the decision, but if necessary, decide what is best for you. For example, it may seem like going to graduate school on the other side of the country for a few years, even if that means being away. The right partner understands and supports you. Ultimately, focusing on your own personality strengthens your connection. This is because they can join each other as fully recognized people rather than defining themselves through relationships.

CHAPTER FOUR

Loyalty

Being unfaithful is perhaps the most harmful thing in any relationship. The combination of love and loyalty is enduring and sacred. Loyalty is a building block of relationships. You have to commit to your partner if you want it to work. Your significant other may not be as resourceful as your co-workers or as outgoing as your ex-boyfriend, but there's a reason you chose them over everyone else. This should be the foundation of your unwavering loyalty. If there is a third party, the relationship fails tremendously, whether you disclose that person's identity or keep it secret from your partner.

Compromise

Compromises by both people are essential for a relationship to thrive. Work on finding common ground between the two of you so that your relationship can flourish. Thinking only of your needs and robbing your partner over and over again can lead to resentment and even end your relationship.

The hurly-burly of everyday life can lead to a slump in your relationship. So it's important to find ways to fill yourself with fun, excitement, and happiness. We don't always have a sun-and-rainbow relationship, but it's important to let the happy times overshadow the unhappy times. If you can face problems together with a smile on your face, you won't fail as a couple. Laughter unites two hearts and drives away all sorrow.

Building Fair Partnerships

There is nothing better than being with a true accomplice. That way, you'll feel like you can handle anything as a couple, no matter what life throws at them. But when the ratios are unequal and only one person makes an effort, things quickly go downhill. To build a long-term relationship, it's important to work on finding a balance between things like housework and emotional support. Indeed, we can help each other and show love by standing up and supporting each other in times of need. But check back often to keep things fair.

In defining a relationship as a whole, love at its core is: Do we want the same? Are we negotiating well? Are we emotionally available? If you keep asking yourself these questions, it won't feel one-sided.

CHAPTER FIVE

Communicate each other's needs

It's perfectly possible to have a great happy relationship with little or no sex if you both want sex or find a way to make it work...but sex is really important to you and if you can't get to the same sexual side no matter what you do, you’re going to have an unhappy period. This brings us back to the idea that your happiness is more important than love. Of course, you can work on your sexual compatibility, but it doesn't matter how much you love your partner if you're tired of trying everything. Doing so is a big problem.

Relationships are not static. As time passes and people and relationships change, you have to accept this for the relationship to last. Talking about sex more often helps you stay connected.

Develop your communication skills

Communication is the driving force of love, without which there can be no true and lasting love. Communication in a relationship is necessary for setting boundaries, expressing love, solving problems, talking about needs, and having good sex. Avoiding difficult topics or focusing too much on relationship issues can cause relationships to fall apart, leading to circular arguments.

This can lead to frustration and resentment. You can have all the love in the world, but good communication is what makes things work in the long run. Stay on the same page in a relationship so you can learn to get through the tough times. Is important

Feeling ready for a relationship

Sometimes the mind is so complicated. You can love someone but you don't want to be with them right now. You may have other goals or feel emotionally unavailable. No, you may not be ready to commit. Once more, timing matters. When things feel a little weird, having a conversation with your partner about what you want and where you're at in the long run can help you understand if what you have is really working. Every relationship is different and many problems are solvable. But love, while wonderful and obviously necessary, is not the only ingredient in a healthy relationship, nor (arguably) the most important one.

CHAPTER SIX

Conclusion

All successful relationships require intentional effort from both sides to make things work.

Many couples give up when they encounter minor conflicts along the way and adopt a few simple strategies and changes.

The best way to experience growth together is to learn from each other every day and show your willingness to be better for each other.

Sure, each person may have their own needs and interests, but it's always beneficial to agree on what works as a team. In the absence of consensus, this can become a breeding ground for problems.

www.ingramcontent.com/pod-product-compliance
Lightning Source LLC
LaVergne TN
LVHW020532160826
845677LV00015B/4019

* 9 7 9 8 8 4 8 1 5 2 6 3 0 *